Ken Hildrew's
EXMOOR

Ken Hildrew's
EXMOOR

KEN HILDREW

HALSGROVE

First published in 2002 by Halsgrove

British Library Cataloguing-in-Publication Data
A CIP record for this title is available from the British Library

ISBN 1 84114 188 7

HALSGROVE

Halsgrove House
Lower Moor Way
Tiverton, Devon EX16 6SS
Tel: 01884 243242
Fax: 01884 243325
email: sales@halsgrove.com
website: www.halsgrove.com

Printed in Hong Kong by Regal Printing Company

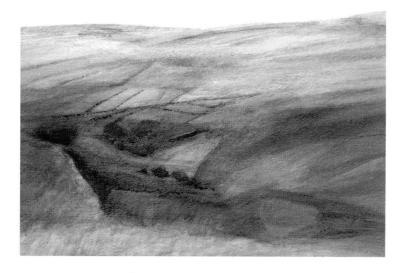

Contents

To lovers of Exmoor past, present and future – I humbly dedicate this book.

Acknowledgements

Thanks to Caroline Doyle for typing up my garbled ramblings and making sense out of nonsense; R. & J. Photography for their expertise with digital photography in producing the transparencies for the plates; David Parry for framing the paintings; Julie Abbot of the Old Blacksmith's Gallery in Dulverton for putting on the exhibition and all her support in the past; and to J.M.W. Turner, whose paintings have been my constant inspiration.

In recent years I have come to use acrylic paint as my chosen medium. It is not an exaggeration to say that the development of acrylic paint is the greatest technical breakthrough in five-hundred years. What I find so exciting is the versatility of the paint, giving me a greater range of effects. It is this remarkable versatility which enables me to adapt it to a greater variety of painting techniques. It can be used as a watercolour to create wet effects with the same fluid spontaneity as traditional watercolours, or mixed with an acrylic medium to produce overlays of transparent colour used like oil colour to produce thick impasto textures. It is also ideal for collage painting. Acrylic gel is an ideal adhesive for all manner of materials used in collage and of course we must not forget in all this the drying time; acrylic paint dries very quickly, enabling layers of paint to be applied rapidly which dry to a strong and durable film.

Much has been written about Exmoor over the years, immortalised in R.D. Blackmore's *Lorna Doone* through to contemporary writings. I much admire the work of Hope Bourne who has lived most of her life on the moor and probably knows more than anybody about the precious wilderness. The poems written by Mollie Hawcutt who lives in North Molton I find very moving. Her poem 'Under Winstitchen' is as close to painting with words as you can get (page 35).

Ken Hildrew

My most vivid memories of childhood are dominated by the war, having been born on 18 September 1934 in Woolwich, south-east London. Living so close to the Woolwich Arsenal we were continually being bombed. At the age of seven I spent much of my time in the shelter at the bottom of the garden so to while away the long hours my brother and I used to draw by candlelight. As we had no paper as such, we used the back of wallpaper and cardboard from cereal packets. When the raids finished all the kids in our street would go out and collect shrapnel and spent cannon shells and cases. This became a sort of currency amongst us, three pieces of shrapnel for one cannon case, and any piece of metal that had German writing on, or any writing on, you could name your own price.

When the Blitz, as it was called, was at its height, my parents decided that evacuation was the best answer but even this proved unexpectedly hazardous. The day before we were due to leave a daylight raid meant a rush for the shelter and on the way down the garden I was tripped up by our dog, banging my face on the entrance to the shelter. I looked a very sorry sight the next day: a large lump on my forehead, grazes on my cheek and a split lip. However, we still had to go. We were all packed into coaches with our labels attached to our jackets and gas masks in boxes, together with some packed sandwiches. We were driven to Abbeywood Station and then by train to London Euston. From there we journeyed all through the day to Lancashire. Our final destination was a small village named Cherrytree, close to the Pennines. I can still remember to this day the misery of waiting in the village hall with all the other children while people came in and chose who they would take. As the day drew on my brother and I looked like being the only ones not to be taken. He blamed me, of course, for the sorry state I was in. But as the committee were in a huddle to decide what was best to become of us, two old ladies appeared and we were saved. They took us home to their Edwardian red-bricked house and that became our home for eighteen months.

We soon settled into our new home. Who wouldn't, with real chips, home-baked bread and Eccles cakes – wonderful! On the dining room wall was a large picture of a lioness with some cubs. It was the first time I had ever seen such a large picture in its gilt frame. I spent many hours looking at it and set about copying it. Auntie Bella encouraged me in my efforts and bought me some crayons and a drawing book. I often wondered about that picture and many years later I saw a reproduction in a book of a similar painting by Albert Huggins, an artist from Liverpool in the Victorian age.

Another of my abiding memories of this time was being woken up at 5a.m. each day by hundreds of mill girls going to work. The sound of them singing softly and the clatter of their clogs on the cobbled street remains with me to this day.

Being so close to the Pennines we would be taken on long walks, usually on a Sunday afternoon. I think this must have been my first introduction to a landscape of open hills and large skies uncluttered by buildings. This was to have a profound influence on my later paintings.

After eighteen months we returned to London with distinct Lancashire accents and clogs, which my family found very amusing. Our return home proved to be premature as the V1 and V2 rocket attacks began. These were very frightening – the noise of those rockets coming over and then the silence before the explosion really was bad news. But we managed to survive the remainder of the war despite being bombed out twice. I was eleven years old when the war finally ended and I was able to continue what had been up until then a fairly patchy education, as most schools that I had been going to were either bombed out or being used for some other purpose such as hospitals.

At this time in my life I became an avid collector. I collected anything I could from birds' eggs, birds' feathers, butterflies, beetles, owl pellets – which were very interesting! – cigarette cards, anything. I had boxes and boxes full of everything – it drove my mother mad!

I obtained a place at the Woolwich School of Art, which was annexed to Woolwich Polytechnic, and began my formal training in art. I must confess to being a below-average student, not working particularly hard but just enjoying the less formal atmosphere of the school. I did receive encouragement at Parrot Road Primary School from my aptly-named art teacher, Mr Painter, but mostly it seemed that everyone wished I could be a whizz at technical drawing and woodwork like my brother. Art was not talked about like it is today, especially in the working-class society I came from. So my parents did little to encourage me. To them art was something enjoyed by a few and had nothing to do with the real world. My end-of-term reports only served to reinforce their doubts that I had no future in art and the sooner I got a proper job, the better.

One of the lessons taught me in art school was the importance of drawing, something I understand is still done today and something in which I am a great believer. Many people think

Picasso did silly pictures of women with their eyes in their navels but his sketches prove that he could draw. He was a genius. I remember we spent hours doing pencil or charcoal drawings of plaster statues taken from the sculptures of Michaelangelo, and life drawing in the studio. We were also encouraged to go out sketching.

Being so close to the River Thames gave us the opportunity to draw a subject alive with activity. At this time in its long history the Thames was still a busy working river. Freighters were coming in from all over the world to the King George V Dock or the Royal Albert Docks. Tugs, lighters and sailing barges and the occasional sailing ship were still to be seen. I spent hours going back and forth across the Woolwich free ferry. By doing this you became a part of the whole scene crossing the river, the giant paddles of the ferry churning up the water. I absorbed the whole atmosphere.

At weekends and holidays my mate John Keith and I would go into the marshes that stretched from Plumstead to Gravesend, mile upon mile of reed beds and mudflats. The hours spent roaming this landscape instigated, I believe, my love of wilderness which lasts to this day. I suppose I fell in love with Exmoor for the same reason, a deep affinity with wilderness and desolation. I love the loneliness and the silence.

I remember we built a den at the back of a rusting corrugated football stand. I learned later that this small ground was where Woolwich Arsenal played their home matches before moving to North London and dropping the Woolwich from their title. In this den we kept a small frying pan. We would have some lard or dripping and a couple of slices of bread. Gathering a few gulls' eggs or plovers' eggs we would cook them on a small fire made in a can with holes punched in it. This meal would sustain us all day. Another abiding memory of this period was waiting for the furnace to open at the Ford Motor Works across the river at Dagenham. This usually happened about 4p.m. and in the fading light of winter from a viewpoint at Bostal Woods, which was a high point near to where I lived, this huge gush of flame could be seen for miles and through the river mist the image had a Turneresque feel about it.

Barges in the Thames Estuary
Acrylic 28 x 21in

In its heyday as a working river hundreds of these barges could be seen sailing up and down on the tides.

Dante's Inferno, Dagenham
Acrylic 30 x 24in

As a boy I would stand on the opposite bank of the river to the Ford Motor Works at Dagenham waiting for the furnace to open, releasing a great gush of flame into the sky.

Another favourite haunt of mine was Beresford Square, Woolwich, an open market for fruit and vegetables and a section for fresh fish. I loved to go there and listen to the stall owners shouting their wares. Close by was Manses' Eel and Pie Shop, a marvellous café with marble-topped tables and steam and plenty of atmosphere. A portion of meat pudding, mashed potatoes and peas, a large slice of bread for mopping up the gravy and to finish off with a mug of sweet tea, all for two shillings. I was earning some money after school helping stallholders pack up after a day's trading, which also included a bag of overripe fruit to take home.

It was at art school that I discovered my lifelong love of jazz music. At the bottom end of the street where I lived was Hall's fish and chip shop. A group of us usually went down for 1d worth of chips two or three times a week. Opposite the shop was a row of Victorian houses. From one of them, on occasions, there would come the sound of jazz music. I became intrigued by this and I crept into the front garden and peeked through the curtains. The group of musicians were gathered round a small balding man, with a pipe in his mouth, seated at an upright piano. He was, I learned later, George Webb, largely responsible for the post-war jazz revival in Britain. Other members of the band were Humphrey Lyttelton and Wally Fawkes, whose cartoons appear in newspapers today under the name of Trog.

I purchased my first wind-up gramophone and started my record collection. The first 78 records I bought were Sydney Bechet, the New Orleans soprano sax player, followed by Louis Armstrong and his Hot 5 and Hot 7 recordings. These were made in the 1920s and still remain some of the greatest jazz recordings of all time.

All too soon, I came to the end of my four years of study at art school. I would have preferred to have stayed on and done further studies but my parents made it clear that it was time for me to start earning my keep. After weeks of going to interviews in commercial art studios I got my first paid job in the art department of the *Star* evening newspaper. At this time London was served by three evening newspapers, the *Star*, the *Evening News* and the *Evening Standard*. Two of those have now gone and only the *Standard* remains. I was employed to do numerous jobs in this department, including retouching photographs, drawing maps and diagrams, pasting up the artwork done by Veronica Papworth who was the fashion editor, and also the work of Vicky – the political cartoonist. Vicky was a marvellous charming man and he was a great encouragement to me, teaching me so much about life and painting. During this time, when I was not very busy, I would go into the newsroom and would become what is known as a copy boy, taking typed copy from the journalists into the newsroom for the subeditors – who usually slaughtered it!

The chief subeditor was a giant of a man called Bernard Murphy who chain-smoked Passing Cloud cigarettes. We boys were often sent out to Fleet Street to buy him these. I liked doing this little job because it meant that I could linger in The

Street of Ink which had a lively bustling atmosphere. Sometimes I would go out with the *Star* photographer on an assignment and have to rush back with the film for processing. This meant getting taxis from sometimes as far away as London Airport or one of the smart West End hotels. Often I would use the underground, dodge paying the fare and get the taxi fare on expenses. Dishonest I know, but it supplemented my meagre wages.

After a year in the newspaper business I secured a job in a small commercial art studio in Covent Garden. It was interesting working with illustrators and lettering artists, and I became friends with one of the artists, a chap named Henry Arrowsmith who was a couple of years older than me. He shared my love of jazz music and we used to go to jazz clubs together after work. He certainly knew his way around Soho, and took me to all sorts of pubs and clubs and introduced me to lots of interesting people. He lived with his mother and sister in a flat on the Edgware Road. After a while, to save me from having to rush to get the last train home, I would stay at the flat which meant we could go to all-night jazz sessions and go straight to work in the morning. It was Henry who introduced me to modern jazz through the recordings of Charlie Parker. These were brought into England by Henry's sister's boyfriend who worked on the ships between here and America. There was at this time a group of young English musicians eager to learn this new music, led by the late great Ronnie Scott who later went on to become one of the finest tenor sax players in the world. He eventually opened his own club, mainly for his own use and the use of his friends, but I became a member. I love the atmosphere of jazz clubs. I used to do sketches of the players as they worked, displaying these little sketches and sometimes a finished painting which I had done at home, in a café in Covent Garden close to where I worked.

One day I went in for my lunch to be greeted by a Dutchman who was over from Holland selling flowers. He was a great jazz fan and was hoping to hear some jazz while in England. We took him to a jazz club that night and all had a great time, arranging to meet for lunch the following day. Over lunch he casually remarked about the drawings and said he would like to buy some to take home, not knowing that I was the artist, but Henry soon put him right. When he asked me how much I wanted for them I was flabbergasted that somebody wanted to buy my work. I was happy to give them to him but he insisted on paying. So on that day I sold my first pieces of art for ten shillings each which was a lot of money in those days. This was it, I thought, I am on my way!

But my euphoria was short-lived for not long after this I got my call-up papers and found myself in the uniform of the Royal Air Force. I shall never forget the first few days after arrival at boot camp, boy oh boy! The way the camp barber relished my carefully groomed hair with the 'DA' at the back! 'How would you like it this morning, sir?' he said jovially. 'Oh,' I said, 'just a light trim on top, and a wash and blow dry!' Whoosh! Off it all came. Years of careful coiffure lay on the floor. I was devastated. I felt pretty much the same about the attitude of

Thames Mist at St Paul's
Acrylic 18 x 20in

When I worked in Fleet Street I often paused on Blackfriars Bridge to observe St Paul's Cathedral through the mist.

our drill corporal, a large Welsh gentleman called Price. He made it very clear to all of us who had come from London that we were not his favourite people. I was not used to this prejudice but despite him I found my new way of life, although harsh at times, quite enjoyable. Being in a billet with 30 other blokes from all over the British Isles was very enlightening and very, very funny. The banter and the jokes that went on were absolutely great. I do feel sorry for lots of young boys today who have missed out on National Service. It certainly did me no harm.

After doing my training at a station just outside Blackpool, I was posted briefly to Market Drayton in Shropshire. It was a vehicle maintenance depot and I worked in the paint shop! Being a professional artist the RAF thought that was the best place for me. I was signwriting notice boards most of the time. In charge of our section was Flight Sergeant Hooper, a cunning man from Liverpool. He was not too strong at discipline and I found out very quickly that he was a keen ornithologist, and thereafter spent many hours in his lovely warm office, drinking tea and talking about birds. When I was on leave I did some small watercolours for him, bird studies, which he was very pleased with. He never paid me but I got the occasional seventy-two-hour pass which was worth its weight in gold. But I was only at Market Drayton for three months when I got a posting to Gibraltar. Once more I was devastated that my life was going to be turned upside down again. Flight Sergeant Hooper, however, was very envious telling me that Gib was a dream posting. After two weeks' embarkation leave I reported to RAF Lyneham and with 60 other airmen I flew out to Gibraltar and Spain.

Disembarking from the aircraft on that very hot July day I had mixed emotions. The first thing that struck me was the heat. I had never come across anything like it before in all my life; it was over 90° and not something to experience in the thick serge uniform we had left England in ten hours before. The light was blinding; everything seemed to shimmer in the heat. I staggered under the wing of the Hastings transport plane that had borne us laboriously from England, thankful for the shade. I was able to focus better on my surroundings.

The colour of everything was such a contrast to what I had been used to, much more primary. I had grown up in a more subtle northern light filtered by mists and cloud. This was the light of Van Gogh and Cézanne, mine belonged to Sickert, Constable and Turner. The next thing I saw filled me with some joy; dozens of kites circling lazily on some scrubland next to the runway – this was a good start, I thought – plenty more of this to come.

After a couple of weeks settling in at RAF Devil's Tower, which was the name of my new posting, I got to know my new surroundings and mates. I then took my first trip into Spain. I was fortunate to have in my room a chap who had been on the Rock for a year, so he agreed to hold my hand, as it were. In those days you had to have a visa to get into Spain; it cost 7s 6d for three visits and your passport was stamped 'entrada' on entry and 'salida' on return. This was Spain as it was before the mass package-holiday boom. It was a country still feeling the effects of a dreadful civil war and living under a restrictive and somewhat brutal regime. Food was still desperately short and Spain was just coming out of what was known as 'Los años de hambrey' – the years of hunger. Despite all the deprivation, especially in Andalucia, and the shortage of food and work, there was still a vibrance about the people, who were eager to know you. We would catch a bus from La Linea to Malaga, stopping at a small fishing village called Marbella. We usually arrived round about lunchtime and would have sardines grilled on an open fire on the beach.

There were a number of Spanish workers employed on the station. Our section had eight, whose tasks included keeping the station cars washed down, the hangar floors clean and generally making things tidy. These tasks were supposed to be dished out daily by a corporal in charge of our section. Coming from Newcastle upon Tyne, he was football potty and had no time or inclination to dish out these jobs. We did a deal whereby if there was a match on between our station team and the Army or Navy, he would disappear and I would cover for him, which meant that I was left to make sure that the Spanish lads were kept busy. I had them gardening, whitewashing buildings and helping me with my signs which were done in both Spanish and English. In my spare time when they were having their lunch break I used to sketch them while they ate their packed lunches of chorizo sausage, which was hard as biltong, some bread and rough red wine drunk from leather wine skins which they offered me most of the time. I refused the sausage but didn't mind the wine. They nicknamed me 'el pintor' – the painter.

One day they were all in a state of high excitement. All the major towns and villages in Spain had their annual 'feria' – fiesta – and in Algeciras, which was across the bay from Gibraltar, one of the boys had a nephew who was to appear for the first time in the bullring as a torero. Although I had seen the posters around advertising the corridas I had never been to one. They asked me to join them the following Sunday, so I did and there began my lifelong interest and love of the fiesta.

I bought a quarter-share in an old car, a Jowett Javelin. We bought it from a chap returning to England. We tarted her up with a respray and I made a set of seat covers with fabric left over from doing up the interior of the Air Officer Commanding's Dakota aircraft. On weekends and leave the four of us would set off to explore Spain in much the same way immortalised by Laurie Lee. Having our own transport meant we could go off the main roads, such as they were, and find the more remote villages. The inhabitants would be totally gobsmacked at our arrival – even more so when I wandered into the main square to do some drawing. We always took a good supply of cigarettes and sweets on these trips. We would go into a bar which soon filled up with people curious at our strange accents. Conversation with the locals was somewhat fractured, they simply had no idea of the outside world. I remember on one occasion a man came forward saying that he was able to speak English. Great, we thought, and we asked him to say something – he grinned and said 'Winston Churchill' and that was it, that was all he knew. We would order jugs of wine and tapas which were usually squares of bread with goats' cheese, very, very crude because food was still very hard to come by. The cigarettes proved popular. They would be handed round and examined closely. The children clambered for the sweets which we tossed at them through the window of the bar.

On some occasions we drove straight to some of the big cities – Seville, Cordoba, Granada and Jerez. On one trip to Seville we decided to go to a flamenco show. We were advised by the owners of our pension that the best show to see was at the Hotel Christina. We duly arrived in our best bibs and tuckers and got a good table. The show was indeed good; wonderful music and tremendous atmosphere, beautiful dancing girls, what more could you want? But the highlight of this particular evening for me was that I nearly danced with Brigitte Bardot. Between shows the floor was used for dancing. We noticed BB in the audience and for a dare I thought I would ask her to dance. Goaded on by the others and full of Pimms No. 1, I approached her table. I got quite close but at the last minute I was stopped by a large gentleman who stood between me and her table, and very politely informed me that Miss Bardot was not dancing tonight! For a brief moment she glanced up – did she smile I asked myself on the way back to the table? I like to think she did.

Another time, in Seville, we met up with a bunch of seamen from Liverpool who had taken over the upstairs room of a restaurant and were throwing a party. I can remember a traffic cop coming in for a quiet drink after work and getting so drunk he fired his revolver into the ceiling as a party trick!

These were wonderful times for me but all good things come to an end. My tour of Gib was over. It was back home and demob. In the last period of my service I met Norman Kyte who was to remain a close friend to this day.

After leaving the Air Force I could not settle down and I was job-hopping, not staying in the same place for very long. I decided I would go back to Spain so I sold what I could, borrowed some money from my mother and got a single train ticket and left. After a month I was joined by a friend from art school. I must point out that this friend was female, and very attractive, and later went on to become a successful model. She flew out and I met her in Gibraltar and for ten months we roamed around until the money ran out. We just had enough for two tickets on a Castle Liner, sharing a cabin with four others in steerage. We docked at Tilbury after four days to be met by her mother who was shocked at our appearance. I had not noticed how bedraggled we had become. But I knew now I had to start to do some serious work. I had no money, indeed I owed people money, and I had no job. I decided that I wanted to live in London and so I left home and went to live with Norman Kyte and his wife Lyn.

Olive Trees near Priego de Cordoba, Spain
Acrylic 24 x 20in

Priego de Cordoba in central Andalucia in Spain is a vast arid area, a hot landscape in every sense of the word. Priego is one of the biggest producers of olive oil in Spain.

I soon secured a job in the display department of Saxone Lilley & Skinner, the shoe company. It was interesting work and I enjoyed it very much. I stayed there for a couple of years and then went as a studio manager to a small printing company, Turner Studios, owned by two wonderful people, Arron and Moisha Lubofski. It was a small firm of silk-screen printers producing posters and show cards for such diverse clients as Green Shield Stamps, the Ford Motor Company and the Ministry of Information. One of the layout artists there was a chap called Shaun, a keen boxing fan, and we often used to go to the boxing at Bethnal Green and then along for a nice late-night ruby (curry). He later landed a job in Hollywood working at the Walt Disney studios.

Moisha Lubofski was a keen painter who had taken a course of lessons with Victor Passmore. I persuaded her that we should do a series of abstract limited-edition prints for the art market which we did. The experience I gained from producing these prints enabled me at a later date to set up my own printing shop to produce prints for hotels. Turner Studios relocated to a Victorian warehouse in Pentonville. Arron Lubofski decided that the rent being asked for one of the floors was far too high so he bought the whole building and became the landlord. There was a service flat in the building which he asked me to take over so that I could keep an eye on the building at night and at the weekends. Since it was rent-free I agreed to do this and it meant that I could use the studio to do my paintings. It also allowed me to save enough money to put down on our first house. By this time I was married and we decided we needed a garden for our daughter Sherry, who was growing fast.

My next move was to Hayes in Middlesex, to a job with Waitrose, the supermarket branch of the John Lewis Partnership, at their headquarters at Greenford. Julius Englert, the display manager, introduced me to the artist, Felix Topolski, who had a marvellous studio under the arches of Waterloo Station. I went there several times to show him how to do silk-screen printing. He was at this time producing his own limited-edition newspaper, the *Topolski Chronicle*, and wanted to introduce some colour into the illustrations. By way of a thank-you he gave me some copies of his paper which I reluctantly later sold to raise much-needed funds. After some years I heard on a radio programme that copies of the same paper had sold for thousands at auction. C'est la vie! I felt very much at home in the creative atmosphere of his studio. It was always being visited by the most amazing people and I felt it was about time for me to think about getting some serious painting done. My work at this time was selling regularly from galleries and I felt confident enough to try to make a living from painting full-time. It was while I was making these plans that I was offered a job in television in the design department at Thames Television Studios, Teddington. I decided to go for it and put becoming a full-time painter on hold for a while.

There followed several years working on programmes as diverse as *Pinky and Perky*, *Opportunity Knocks*, the *Benny Hill Show* and the *Tommy Cooper Show*, together with major dramas to name but a few. Tommy Cooper was a lovely person, not at all showbizzy like so many of them. He was always full of fun and jokes. One of the senior designers was Fred Pusey who had been an art director with Alexander Korda, the film producer. He had worked on films like *Fire Over England*, *The Private Lives of Henry VIII* and *The Shape of Things to Come*. It was he who taught me to look below the surface of things for that which remains unseen but is just as important as that which is seen. 'You have to use your inner eye,' he said. I always remember this and I have carried this philosophy into my paintings today.

I finally left television and moved with my family to Crowborough in East Sussex. I had now begun to paint virtually full-time the landscapes of the Ashdown Forest and the Weald of Kent. A gallery in London started to sell my paintings of the Thames I knew as a lad, which were bought for

corporate collections of city banks, financial institutions insurance companies and the like. I was also producing my limited-edition silk-screen prints which I was selling to hotels through an agent. I was continuing to visit Spain, usually with my dear friend, Tony Allen, whom I had met some years previously. Our mutual love of jazz music and the bulls drew us together. Tony is a drummer of some repute and through him I have met many jazz musicians. They treat me as one of their own and I take that as a great compliment.

I was invited to go to Salamanca one year, a very elegant city. I was so impressed with it that the following year I went with Tony. I took him down to the River Tormes and across the Roman bridge to look back at the city. The look on his face told me he felt the same way I did. We have been going back regularly for many years and have made many, many friends there. We have become known simply as 'los dos' – a Spanish expression that literally speaking means the two – by all those people whom we have got to know over the years.

Below the North Downs, Kent
Acrylic 20 x 15in

A typical Kentish landscape with oast houses. These very attractive buildings are fast disappearing from the landscape. Used for drying hops, those that are left are now converted into homes.

PRIVATE COLLECTION

I remember on one of our visits walking down the main street towards the Plaza Major. All of a sudden I stopped dead in my tracks. Coming towards us was the famous ventriloquist Señor Wenses. I remember him years ago on television. As he came close I made my hand into the shape of a face. 'It's you,' I said, 'the world-famous Señor Wenses.' He stopped and said with a smile, 'Thank you for remembering me. I have been retired for many years.' We reminisced for a while and then his daughter said he must go home for a rest. This and many other occasions make Salamanca a very special place for us. As I write in 2002, it has been designated the European City of Culture and I hope to be there again in September, exhibiting and taking part in the celebrations.

There now comes a turning point in my life. My wife and I drifted apart, something that I was wholly responsible for, and I moved down to the West Country in 1984 to start a new life. It was time for me to put into my paintings all I had learned over the past years and I realised that the landscapes of Exmoor would be my means of doing it. From my early years as a boy wandering over the marshes, to my time spent in the vast landscapes of Spain, all of these experiences I would use in creating my paintings of wilderness Exmoor. Here I had continual inspiration on my doorstep: wilderness, luminosity of light and the colours of Sickert, greys, greens, browns and ochres. I just fell in love with the area.

Fortunately, shortly after moving down to Devon, I secured a commission to paint a large panel to go in the Orient Express ferry which sailed between Venice and Istanbul. The panel measured 8ft by 27ft and had to be painted in sections. The weather was, thankfully, kind to me and I was able to use the back garden of the cottage where we then lived in Brayford. I never saw the finished work in situ but several years later I was taking part in an exhibition in Southsea. I had sold one of my Thames paintings to a couple who were at the bar having a drink with me and I was telling them about the commission for the ferry boat. The barman interrupted to say that he had been a purser on the ship and described to us exactly where the panel was. Another man came into the bar and started chatting. We were introduced and we started to talk about paintings, particularly marine paintings. After a while we were interrupted by a phone call for him. He excused himself curtly and disappeared and left in a hurry. The next time I saw him he was on television being interviewed from Zeebrugge. He was chief of diving at Portsmouth and had gone to the ferry disaster when the *Spirit of Free Enterprise* had capsized.

Salamanca Cathedral, Spain
Acrylic 28 x 21in

It is over forty years since I first saw the Cathedral from across the River Tormes. If you drive to Salamanca you can see the Cathedral rising above the city 20 miles away.

Spanish Bulls grazing near Salamanca
Acrylic 20 x 30in

This painting was on show at the international exhibition in Salamanca in September as part of the European City of Culture.

Techniques, teaching and the Exmoor effect

I continued to work on steadily building up my reputation in local galleries, having one-man shows and taking part in mixed exhibitions and carrying out commissions for clients. It is flattering to think that I have a following now. The feedback from customers, knowing that I have sold a painting to someone who really wants it, is very rewarding. One lady who lives on Exmoor, who was very active but cannot do so much now, told me that her collection gets her through the long winter days. Each time she looks at a painting afresh she finds something new. That means a lot to me.

I have been around long enough for my work to be widely familiar to many people and in recent years I have also been teaching. But when I am conducting

a class I try not to overpower my students with my style. Imitation and pastiche do not make good art. I encourage them to develop their own style. I find teaching very rewarding and it makes me go back to basics when talking about perspective, composition, form, colour and texture.

For centuries the recording of nature has preoccupied artists who have been inspired by their environment and the atmospheric changes of the landscape. Living as I do close to Exmoor and surrounded by its intrinsic beauty, my paintings are influenced by the environment. I often choose a small area of a landscape to paint, using the same landscape again and again, selecting my own sky to suit the mood. I try to capture the moods and the stillness, the loneliness of the moor. I prefer it in winter. I see a particular light come across the sky and think 'that would look tremendous up on Molland Common'. I might do sketches or just sit and look at it, chase the light, see how it changes. The vastness of the moor can provide a diverse number of different landscapes ever changing through the year. Every artist has his own technique developed over years of work. It becomes very much his own handwriting, something that becomes purely his own. I make it a practice to rearrange the components of a landscape if by doing so I can enhance the whole composition. By adding or taking away, it is possible to make an ordinary painting into something special.

I like my light to be veiled – reminiscent of those Turneresque mists on the Thames – and over the years I have developed a palette that I find particularly suited to the Exmoor landscape. I never use black, preferring to mix my own and finding that black pigments dull out other colours. My preferred palette is as follows:

Titanium white
Naples yellow
yellow ochre
golden ochre
cadmium yellow
deep cadmium red
raw sienna
burnt sienna
raw umber
burnt umber
ultramarine blue
cerulean blue
olive green
flesh tint
deep violet
bronze yellow
Payne's grey.

I am often asked who are my main influences, a very difficult question to answer because over the years the work of many artists has had a profound influence on me. J.M.W. Turner remains a constant source of inspiration. He was a supreme painter of light and its effect on the landscape. Other painters I admire are Whistler – his Thames paintings are sublime, using oil paint very, very thinly, letting the texture of the canvas show through. Critics said that these paintings would not last and would disappear in time and accused him of throwing a pot of paint in the face of the public! I try to keep an open mind regarding all painting and I do admire good abstract art. The paintings by Mark Rothko, the American artist, are beautiful and serene canvasses. I am a traditional painter of pictures but I like to think there is an element of abstraction in my work because I am not a mirror-image painter; I like to get to the bones of a landscape.

I have always been interested in wildlife, ever since I was a boy. Although I rarely put animals or birds in my paintings I sometimes see something that interests me enough to put it in:

The River Thames at Dusk
Acrylic 28 x 21in

Lambeth looking down towards the Upper Pool circa 1950. A painting evoking memories of the river that I knew as a boy.

a barn owl, perhaps, quartering a field; a stag on the moor; young foxes chasing butterflies; a buzzard soaring over the moor. I once saw 18 buzzards soaring over Brayford church one Sunday afternoon – luckily I was with some friends and we were all able to count them. We have recently put some of the garden at my present home, Malt House down to wild flowers. The first year we had a flush of poppies, but subsequently nothing. The number of wild birds that come into the garden as a result of the wild-flower patch is very rewarding. Goldfinches, bullfinches, long-tailed tits, gold-crested wrens, tree creepers, all manner of birds, and very regularly a visit from a marauding sparrowhawk.

An artist should always look for a dominant feature in his composition. In my case it is Bampfylde Clump, a ring of trees on a hill close by North Molton where I live. These trees form a landmark on the horizon for miles around yet retain an air of mystery. I have painted them many times and in many ways – at different times of the day and through the seasons of the year. Although Exmoor is primarily the major subject of my paintings, I do from time to time paint different landscapes as a deterrent from getting too stale. The Somerset Levels are a good source of subject for me, with the lines of pollarded willows and reflections of trees in flooded fields. A recent journey to Scotland to visit friends also resulted in a trip through the Highlands. I was totally enthralled by the craggy heights of the mountains and the vast lochs. But I never tire of Exmoor; I'm happy here, rejoicing in this wonderful, wonderful landscape.

In recent years my method of working has developed to suit my way of painting. That is not to say that it is rigid and inflexible. I use drawings and watercolours done in situ and then return to the studio to produce a finished painting. I have found that working outdoors painting 'plein air' pictures, I become bogged down with what I consider irrelevant detail. I try in my paintings to capture the abstract quality of the landscape which is felt as well as seen. Fortunately an artist's vision is his own and no one can borrow his eyes or his soul.

In the modern world of instant communication with text messages, faxes, e-mail and www.com I often wonder what rôle the visual artist now has in this modern technology. All through history artists have been communicators and from the first paintings scratched and rubbed on cave walls 40,000 years ago up to the present day we have endeavoured to leave our mark – a personal statement which says who we are. When I am asked about painting and how it is done or why it is done, I am afraid that some of my answers may appear to be rather glib! I have always refused to use 'art speak' – a language used by critics and intellectuals when talking or writing about art. Turner was once asked about painting and his only reply was 'that it's all a rum do' and that's good enough for me. I prefer to let my paintings speak for themselves and in doing so, if they convey to the viewer something about nature and how it affects me, then I think they have succeeded. We should all ignore the dogmas surrounding art today. Too much is written about what is fashionable and we are confronted with never-ending lists of clichés and art terms as we move through impressionism, post-impressionism, expressionism, futurism, pop art, abstract, action painting through to conceptualism, the list seems endless. Perhaps I am out of step with many of today's ideas, put forward by pundits who write endless essays on what separates good art from bad. I have spent over fifty years endeavouring to capture the boundless subjects provided by nature and hope, on the journey, I have produced through my paintings some pleasure to those who look at them.

The Paintings

UNDER WINSTITCHEN

Below me now I glimpse the river
winding through a shallow cleft
Here, I trace the bones of the moor
the skin of earth is tightly stretched
Now brackens tall and turves are reedy
it seems to me the moor takes breaths
as it lies here untamed, seductive
savage curves yet unpossessed

Mollie Hawcutt

Judith McCarthy

Exmoor Hedgerow
Acrylic 14 x 25in

Hedgerows like this can be seen all over the moor. Man and nature combined have, over countless years, produced a wonderful living sculpture.

The Wild Meadow
Acrylic 21 x 28in

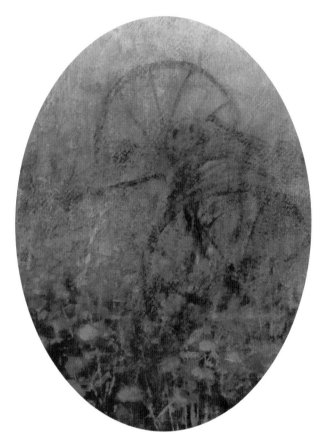

Left to its own devices, nature takes
advantage of 'set aside'

Looking across to Holdridge from the Studio
Acrylic 28 x 21in

A dramatic evening sky above a landscape I can call my own, being so close to Malt House. I was interested in the tattoo of tractor-tyre marks in the middle distance, adding to the composition.

The Silver Thread
Acrylic 24 x 18in

The River Barle winds its way across the moor.

Study for an Exmoor Stag
Watercolour 12 x 10in

A detail of a noble stag. An exercise to try to capture the posture of the magnificent animal in its environment.

Orchard
Acrylic 28 x 24in

I have always been interested in orchards. I love the shape of the old trees made by years of pruning. Alas many varieties have now disappeared altogether with lovely names like Bartletts Glory, Hoary Morning, Taunton Nonpavid, Beauty of Worlds, Fair Maid of Taunton, Slack ma girdle and Devon Crimson Queen; now all but memories.

The Doone Valley
Acrylic 28 x 21in

On Brendon Common
Acrylic 28 x 24in

Simplicity in all things is the secret of the wilderness and one of its most valuable lessons. When in the wilds we must not carry our problems with us or the joy is lost.

Sigard Olsen

Exmoor Landscape near Luccombe
Acrylic 28 x 24in

Porlock
Watercolour 24 x 14in

The ancient weir at Porlock is bathed in a silver light from the veiled sunset.

View from Sandyway
Acrylic 30 x 20in

Molland Common
Acrylic 28 x 21in

Winter Snow, Bampfylde
Acrylic 20 x 10in

A dramatic change in the weather again illustrates how snow transforms the landscape.

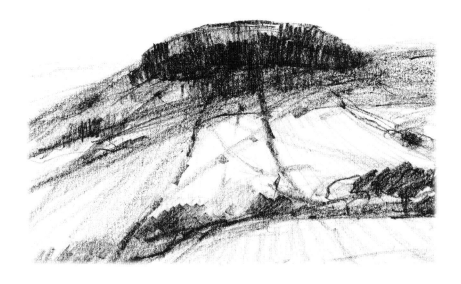

Bampfylde Clump
Acrylic 24 x 18in

A low-key landscape showing the Clump dominating the composition.

Mineral Landscape
Acrylic 30 x 20in

At Brayford there are huge quarries, some parts of which have now been closed down and with the passing of time nature is claiming back its own; grasses and heather are appearing, trees are once more becoming established. It is a haunt for wildlife and if you are lucky you can see a peregrine.

Rock Forms, Heddon's Mouth
Acrylic 30 x 20in

A semi-abstract painting depicting the wonderfully dramatic effects of erosion caused by the sea and time.

Soaring Buzzards
Acrylic 28 x 24in

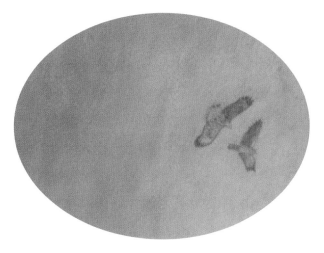

After a hot day the sun has set on the moor and a pair of
buzzards take to the sky to perform their mating flight
soaring in the thermals. Talons locking they fall towards
the earth and then part and start again. It is a sensuous
tango; the sky is their ballroom, the wind their orchestra.

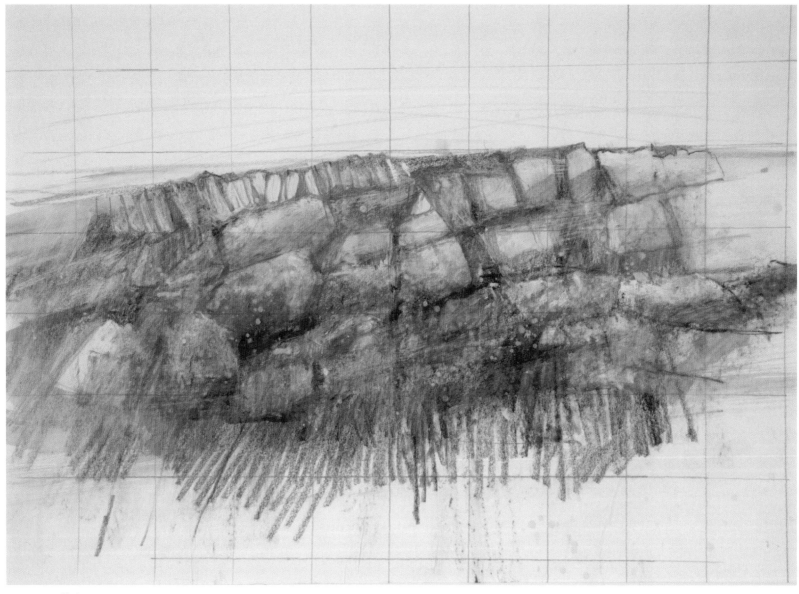

Ancient Wall, first state

A pencil-and-wash drawing of the stonework.

Ancient Wall, second state

I use a combination of collage and paint in endeavouring to capture the many different textures in the wall.

Ancient Moor Wall
Acrylic 28 x 24in

The third state of these wall studies, exploring the theme of grandeur and decay, time and space as expressed in the remains of an ancient wall. I deliberately kept the moor beyond the wall simple to emphasise the texture in the stones.

Woody Bay
Acrylic 14 x 12in

A Patch of Blue
Acrylic 25 x 14in

A break in the clouds brings a promise of better weather to come.

Last Light, Exmoor
Acrylic 24 x 20in

In the last hours of daylight the landscape fuses into soft tones of pink and orange.

Barn Interior
Acrylic 20 x 18in

The contrast between the cool interior stillness of the barn and the harsh daylight; outside all is quiet, save for the twittering of swallows flying in and out to their nests high in the roof.

Barle Valley, Simonsbath
Acrylic 28 x 21in

The River Barle runs through the heart of the moor and will feature in many of my paintings.

Winter at Cornham
Acrylic 24 x 18in

Illustrates the transformation after the snow; the covering up of much ground interest allows highlights and pinpoints to become accentuated and brightened in colour by comparison.

In Fields of Gold
Acrylic 28 x 21in

When I am working in the studio most of the time I listen to music. At the time I was working on this painting I was listening to the late Eva Cassidy singing 'In Fields of Gold' and it seemed to fit.

Huntsmen in the Barle
Acrylic 28 x 24in

After a long day on the moor huntsmen, hounds and horses enjoy a rest in the cool clear water of the Barle near Dulverton.

PRIVATE COLLECTION

Exmoor at Hawkridge
Acrylic   28 x 24in

Snow Shadows
Acrylic on board 20 x 30in

The late-afternoon sun backlights a stand of trees casting long shadows on the snow.

Badgworthy Valley
Acrylic 28 x 24in

Badgworthy is very reminiscent of the glens in Scotland with deep banks of bracken and heather and outcrops of rock.

I am not a topographical painter but seek rather to create an impression of the miraculous secret landscape of hidden Exmoor, its spirit and atmosphere, ever changing through the seasons.

Ken Hildrew, February 2002

Moor Landscape
Acrylic 40 x 32in

In this heavy impasto painting I used palette knives and pieces of card to apply the paint to obtain a rich-textured painting. The surface has been scratched, scraped and overpainted in transparent glazes to achieve the finished effect, illustrating how versatile acrylic can be.

Wells Cathedral
Acrylic 24 x 18in

An impression of the west front of the cathedral bathed in evening sunlight. Wells is a city where I exhibit regularly and I find it a magical place. Though I am not a religious man, I am interested in why men built such great edifices. It is also good to paint subjects other than Exmoor from time to time as then one comes back to the subject refreshed.

Glastonbury Tor from the Levels
Acrylic 24 x 14in

The flat landscape of the Somerset Levels is dominated by the Tor rising up into the sky. A place for pilgrims to contemplate the many legends surrounding the Isle of Avalon.

Reflections in Flooded Fields — the Somerset Levels
Acrylic 24 x 18in

On the way to Wells I pass through the Somerset Levels, another landscape I like to visit whenever I can. Here too is an ancient land full of myths and legends.

Dunster Castle
Acrylic 28 x 18in

North Molton after Rain
Acrylic 28 x 21in

The landscape after heavy rain appears to shine, the wet fields bright with reflective light.

Wild Flowers, Malt House
Acrylic 24 x 14in

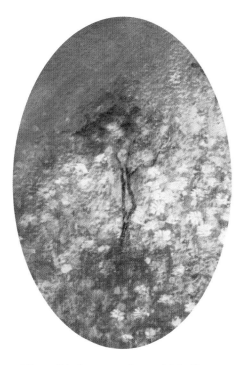

The wild-flower garden at Malt House
helps to create the illusion that there is
no boundary between the garden and
the countryside.

Barle Valley at Cornham Brake, Simonsbath
Acrylic 24 x 18in

The River Barle winds down from Pinkery through Cornham.

East Lyn
Acrylic 28 x 24in

The East Lyn river in full spate roars down over rocks.

Sudden Rain, Exmoor
Acrylic   28 x 21in

A low-horizon picture with the sky being the major part of the composition.

Fading Rainbow, Challacombe
Acrylic 28 x 21in

Sheep at Mole's Chamber
Acrylic 26 x 20in

Out sketching one day sheep came to watch me working. They were my only company in this lonely place.

Wood Edge
Acrylic 24 x 18in

I was interested in the broken textures in the foreground made by tractors, the frozen furrows reflecting the trees.

Clovelly
Acrylic 24 x 18in

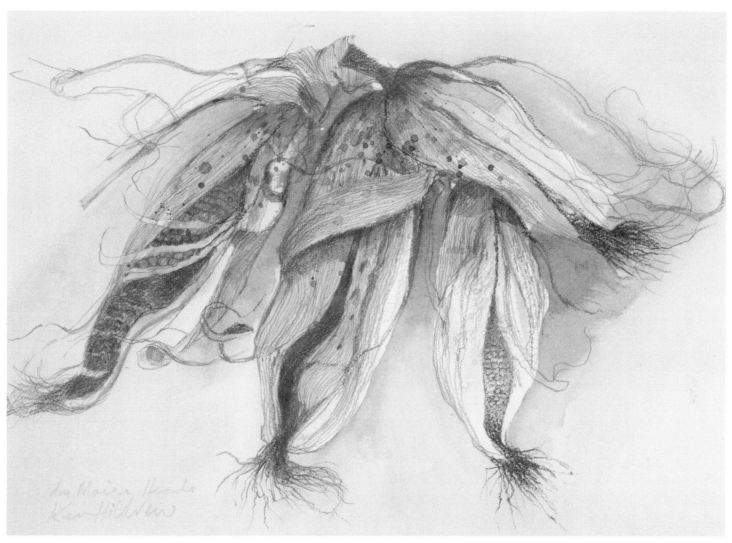

Dried Maize Heads
Pencil drawing with watercolour added

As I was taught at art school about the importance of drawing in the building blocks of any painting, I endeavour to pass this on to my students. I thought the organic quality of the subject lent itself to close observation.

Kingfisher Bridge
Acrylic 25 x 14in

One day I was leaning over a bridge watching brown trout. A kingfisher flashed under the bridge – a magic moment.

The Observer
Acrylic 28 x 21in

Man and bird sharing space in the
cool interior of the barn.

Passing Storm, Exmoor
Acrylic 24 x 18in

A Bright Day, Bampfylde
Acrylic 17 x 12in

A lush landscape in high summer.

Exe Head
Acrylic 25 x 14in

The River Exe rises on the Chains, the most lonely and desolate spot on the whole of Exmoor. The ground is soft and after rain it can become perilous with bogs, and mists that descend without warning.

Holnicote
Acrylic   28 x 18in

White Water and Rocks
Acrylic 28 x 24in

Another painting exploring the theme of rocks and water. Using some collage in this painting helps to convey the textures of the rocks. Their solid mass counterbalances the rush of the water.

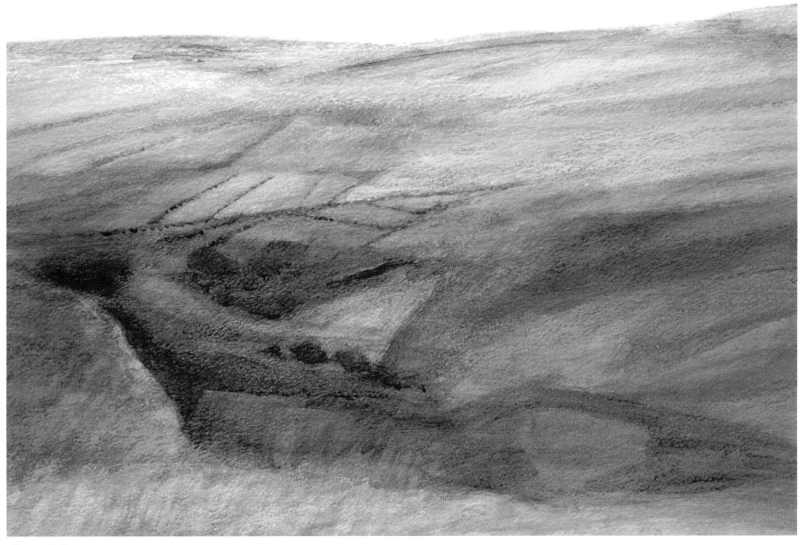

Ilkerton Ridge
Acrylic on canvas 22 x 14in

Moonrise
Acrylic 24 x 14in

An early moon in March rises over Holdridge
illuminating the landscape with its soft light.

The effects of weather and light on the landscape from early spring through summer and autumn to the harsh winter, each season bringing its own beauty.

Ken Hildrew, February 2002

Long Shadows
Acrylic 24 x 20in

I waited until the sun was low on the horizon and casting long shadows across the landscape.

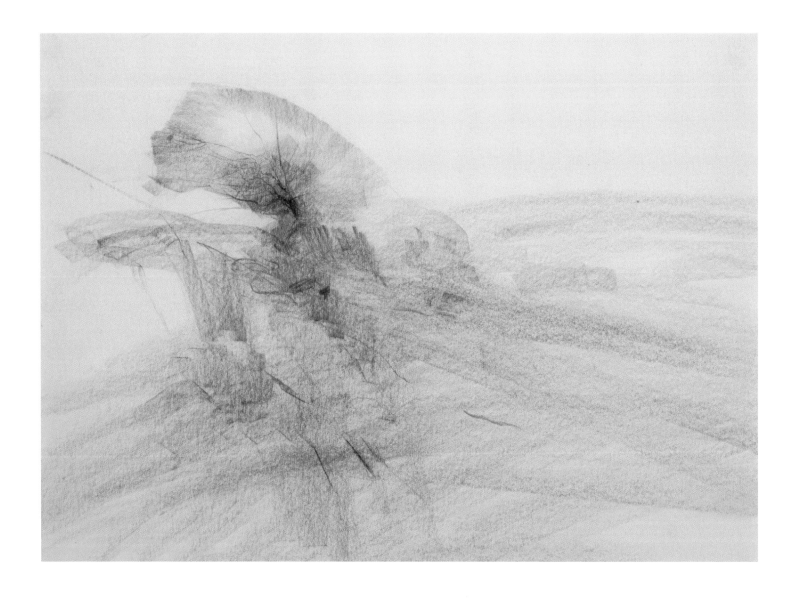

The Blue Tree
Acrylic 28 x 24in

High on the moor a single blackthorn tree bends with the wind, its roots barely clinging to the earth. Branches bleached and wind whipped and yet defiant; a symbol of the harsh struggle against the elements.

The Moor at Anstey Common
Acrylic 20 x 12in

Wild Poppies
Acrylic 14 x 18in

A still life of some poppies taken from
the wild-flower patch at Malt House.

Landacre Bridge
Watercolour 12 x 10in

Landacre Bridge spans the Barle, a favourite playground in the summer
for children who flock to the river on sunny days, to swim and lark about;
best I think in winter when the crowds have gone, leaving it to the
soaring buzzards and wild ponies.

Winter Silence
Acrylic 24 x 18in

Snow fall seems to make landscapes sink into a quietness.

Exmoor Stag
Acrylic 28 x 18in

Drifting Clouds at Challacombe
Acrylic 24 x 18in

A fleeting moment when the sky merges with the landscape.

Crescent Moon, Brendon
Acrylic 28 x 21in

The last of the daylight hovers on the landscape as the moon begins its new cycle.

Riders on the Moor
Acrylic 28 x 24in

A pair of horsemen on the moor at Molland soon
disappear into the mist.

The High Corn Field
Oil 30 x 20in

I came across this corn field being cut and stooked. The timeless quality of the scene made me paint it with a nineteenth-century feel.

Dunkery Beacon
Acrylic 28 x 21in

The highest point on Exmoor. A wonderful vista to which I often return.

Two Moors Way
Acrylic 50 x 40in

By using layer on layer of transparent colours I was able to build up the depth of tone I was after in this painting of the ancient trackway between Exmoor and Dartmoor.

Holdstone Down
Acrylic 12 x 10in

The moor drops into the sea at Holdstone Down.

Arthur Bulled's Pigs
Acrylic 22 x 14in

Arthur Bulled, my neighbour, breeds organic pigs. I often go in one of his barns to witness the birth of piglets and their frantic scramble for their first feed. This again is a subject that I like to paint because I see these pigs in the fields nearby everyday and they are part of my life.

On the King's Nympton–South Molton Road
Acrylic 30 x 20in

The rolling hills of Exmoor on the horizon are the perfect backdrop for this 'busy' landscape in the foreground.

Winter on the Mole
Watercolour 16 x 12in

A lone heron waits by the river hoping for something, anything to come along – pickings are slim at this time of year.

Snow Sky
Acrylic 14 x 12in

A sudden squall of snow transforms the moor in minutes. The wind blows the snow into drifts up against the hedgerows turning the landscape into a mosaic.

The Moor beyond Heasley Mill
Acrylic 20 x 16in

A soft evening sky is reflected in the tones on the moor.

I am often asked by people how long it took to do a certain painting. Time taken to do a painting is irrelevant, I think. Sometimes you can go into a painting and everything flows smoothly. Other times it is a struggle to put anything down — blank brains, the American artist Andrew Wyeth calls it. As for colour or tone I always like to use the analogy of a good snooker player. When you watch a good player at the table he is usually two or three shots ahead of the one he is playing — for me it is the same with painting. I put a colour down knowing that later on by over painting you will arrive at the effect you were after.

Ken Hildrew, February 2002

Coastal Cove
Acrylic 28 x 24in

The coast line of Exmoor has some of the most dramatic cliffs in England, rising sheer 600ft from the sea. The contrast of the strong verticals of the cliff face with the soft humpback horizontals of the moor make for an interesting painting subject.

Longstone Combe
Acrylic 28 x 14in

One of many standing stones that can be seen on Exmoor. A tangible link with our ancient past.

Above the Barle from the Withypool Road
Acrylic 28 x 24in

Barn Gate with Owl
Acrylic 28 x 21in

Winter Light
Acrylic 18 x 10in

An impression of transient light at Bampfylde Clump, one of my favourite subjects.

Tarr Steps, Exmoor
Acrylic 19 x 13in

The medieval packhorse bridge much loved by visitors to the moor.

Lime Trees, Castle Hill
Acrylic 25 x 20in

Road to Dulverton
Acrylic 25 x 14in

On the road to Dulverton stands a group of oak trees, here silhouetted against early-morning mist.

Salisbury Cathedral
Acrylic 30 x 20in

Following in the footsteps of John Constable,
a painting of Salisbury's magnificent Cathedral
rising above the water meadows. Like Wells,
a subject that sets you thinking about the men
who created such magnificent places, and offering
wonderful interplay of sky, light and reflections
in the water; one to refresh the mind on
coming home to Exmoor.

Four watercolour sketches to capture a mood which will be used as aide-memoires in later paintings.

Cow Castle
Acrylic 25 x 14in

Exmoor abounds with barrows and earthworks. Cow Castle is situated on a low hill by a small stream named Whitewater which runs into the Barle near Simonsbath.

At Hoaroak Water
Acrylic 24 x 14in

Culbone Church
Acrylic   25 x 14in

You approach Culbone Church along a coastal path from Porlock, a route trodden by Wordsworth and Coleridge. It is reputed to be the smallest complete church in England.

Porlock Vale
Acrylic 28 x 24in

The vale nestles between the hills and the sea. Some of the best barley in the country is grown in the fields.